Word became Flesh

CHRISTMAS DEVOTIONAL

DAKOTA STEPHENS

Word became Flesh —Copyright ©2024 by Dakota Stephens
Published by UNITED HOUSE Publishing

All rights reserved. No portion of this book may be reproduced or shared in any form–electronic, printed, photocopied, recording, or by any information storage and retrieval system, without prior written permission from the publisher. The use of short quotations is permitted.

All Scripture references included are from the English Standard Version (ESV). Unless otherwise notated. It is recommended to read using this translation for the best use of the devotional.

ISBN: 978-1-952840-72-2

UNITED HOUSE Publishing
Waterford, Michigan
info@unitedhousepublishing.com
www.unitedhousepublishing.com

Cover Layout and Interior Design:
Matt Russell, Marketing Image, mrussell@marketing-image.com

Printed in the United States of America
2024—First Edition

SPECIAL SALES
Most UNITED HOUSE books are available at special quantity discounts when purchased in bulk by corporations, organizations, and special-interest groups. For information, please e-mail orders@unitedhousepublishing.com

To my wife and kids,
This would not have been completed without your unwavering love and support.

Table of Contents

Dec. 1 — In The Beginning 7
Dec. 2 — The True Light 11
Dec. 3 — Beginning of the Narrative 15
Dec. 4 — Zechariah the Priest 19
Dec. 5 — Yahweh has Been Gracious.....................23
Dec. 6 — Zechariah's Unfaithfulness 27
Dec. 7 — Birth of Jesus Foretold..........................31
Dec. 8 — Mary's Submission 35
Dec. 9 — Mary Visits Elizabeth 39
Dec. 10 — Mary's Song of Praise 43
Dec. 11 — Look Upon the Mercy of God.................47
Dec. 12 — The Birth of John the Baptist 51
Dec. 13 — Zechariah's Prophecy Part 1..................55
Dec. 14 — Zechariah's Prophecy Part 2..................59
Dec. 15 — Joseph's Righteousness 63
Dec. 16 — God With Us....................................67
Dec. 17 — The Birth of Jesus Christ......................71
Dec. 18 — Shepherd's and Angels 75
Dec. 19 — Jesus' Birth Proclaimed.......................79
Dec. 20 — Jesus Presented at the Temple 83
Dec. 21 — Behold Our Salvation..........................87
Dec. 22 — Mary Had a Little Lamb 91
Dec. 23 — Anna the Prophetess..........................95
Dec. 24 — Jesus Returns to Nazareth 99
Dec. 25 — Word Became Flesh 103
Notes 107
About the Author 109

DECEMBER 1ST

In The Beginning

Read:
John 1: 1-15

DISCUSS

1. Where else in the Bible are the three words, "In the beginning," used?

2. Why do you think this phrase is important?

3. Do a word study on, "word." What does it truly mean?

4. Verse 3 says, "All things were made through Him." Take a second to look around you and see the beauty of God's creation. What are some things you see?

5. What is special about these words in verse 5: "The darkness has not overcome it."

ANSWERS

1. At the very beginning of the Bible! In Genesis 1:1, "In the beginning God created the Heavens and the Earth."

2. This phrase "in the beginning" helps put into perspective that we are talking about the very beginning of creation, not a random time. That even the word of God was around before anything was created, this points to the word not being created. We will learn more about who the Word is!

3. The Greek word used here is "Logos." What other word is used in the English language that looks like that? Logic! It is rooted in the same Greek word. We see that all "logic," knowledge, and wisdom come from one source, and that is from the Triune God, Creator of heaven and earth and all things therein.

4. Look at the clouds, the grass, the trees, the birds! Watch how they move or appear. Look to what God has created; all these things did not come to existence by chance. All things were divinely created and are being sustained by the author of all life. Take time to talk about the various creations you saw and how they operated.

5. Look at the word "has." This means that the darkness is still trying to overcome the light to this very day, yet it has not and will never prevail. I pray as your family goes through the next twenty-five days, you are protected by God as Satan will try to distract you from studying God's holy word.

TAKEAWAYS

1. "The scope and design of this chapter is to confirm our faith in Christ as the eternal Son of God and the true Messiah and Savior of the world. That we may be brought to receive Him, and rely upon Him, as our prophet, priest, and king, and to give up ourselves to be ruled, and taught, and saved by Him."[1]

2. We cannot seek to fully understand life and the things we face throughout without a Holy God as our grounds of logic and reason. Look upon the marvelous Christ and see the price of our redemption. It is by Christ and Christ alone that we are able to stand and breathe this very day.

3. No matter what you may face, no matter how lost or out of control you may feel, rest assured we have an everlasting peace in Christ, our redeemer. As Jesus carried all burdens through his life as a man and because of His very nature as light of the world, we can lean and press into Christ when all may seem lost and dark. There is always a way. Come to Christ and lay your burdens down at His feet.

DECEMBER 2ND

The True Light

Read:
John 1:6-13

DISCUSS

1. Why was John quick to say he was a witness and not the light?

2. Who is the true light?

3. Why do the Israelites not know or recognize Jesus?

4. How do we receive the right to become children of God?

5. How are the children of God born?

ANSWERS

1. John knew how eager people were to see the Messiah and would follow anyone proclaiming salvation. So, he emphasized he was bearing witness of the coming light and he himself was not the light. He was the heralder of the coming light, Christ Jesus!

2. Jesus! Let us not grow tired of seeking Him in the word of God. We are speaking about the Savior of the world! All of the holy, inspired word of God points to Christ Jesus.

3. The Israelites were looking for a savior to free them from their captivity to Rome. However, Christ did not come riding in triumphantly on a colt, striking down all who opposed. His purpose was bigger than that. Instead, He came humbly in human form as a baby laid in a manger outside of a crowded inn. He was brought into this world surrounded by animals and shepherds, the lowest of them all.

4. Through belief in Him! Romans 10:9-10 states, "Because if you confess with your mouth that Jesus is the Lord and believe in your heart that God raised Him from the dead, you will be saved. For with the heart, one believes and is justified, and with the mouth one confesses and is saved."

5. We are born again not by the will of man or flesh of man, but by the will of God! Look to John 3:1-8 for further study on this question. We must be born again by the Spirit, not by flesh. This is the second birth that is signified by the baptism of true believers in the profession of faith.

TAKEAWAYS

1. In order to see the gates of Heaven, to go unto glory with God the Father forever and ever after death, we must be born again. Not by flesh, but by the spirit.

2. To be a Christian indeed is to believe in Christ's name; it is to agree with the Gospel and have Faith in the one whom the Gospel points to. Not by works alone, but by faith alone, for the glory of God alone.

3. As Christians, we should not boast in ourselves but in the glory of God. May we be quick like John to say we only bear witness to the light; we are not the light. Yet, the light lives and works through us!

DECEMBER 3RD

Beginning of the Narrative

**Read:
Luke 1:1-4**

DISCUSS

1. From this text, who do you think Theophilus is to Luke?

2. What does Luke writing this letter to Theophilus show?

3. Why is it good for us that Luke writes an "Orderly Account"?

4. What do you think Theophilus has been taught about the story of Jesus?

5. Who do you think Luke heard these beginning accounts from?

ANSWERS

1. Theophilus is most likely someone Luke had been sharing the story of Jesus. The term "most excellent," was commonly used to address high-ranking Roman officials. He was likely a Gentile like Luke, someone we could possibly consider a friend.

2. This letter shows us the importance of telling everyone about the Gospel. To share more than a couple sentences and to fully and wholly share the greatest news the world will ever hear. We should follow this example by going out and telling others about this splendid news!

3. We should be grateful that the Lord wholly inspired Luke to write a detailed, ordered account on the life of Christ. Then, we can have "certainty" in the completion of these things about the life of Christ! We have a whole and complete story.

4. Theophilus had probably been told the story of Christ several times. That is why he is now receiving a detailed account. There may have been some questions that he had that can now be answered through a thorough account.

5. When you step back and think about it, Luke was likely around the same time as Christ! So, the information that he has been given is from those eyewitnesses from the beginning. We can surmise that he has heard these things from Mary, Joseph, and Jesus Himself!

TAKEAWAYS

1. "All scripture is breathed out by God and profitable for teaching, for reproof, for correction, and for training in righteousness," - 2 Timothy 3:16, ESV. God's word is perfect and never fails. There is a reason for every single word, sentence, and syntax. They all point to the glory and holiness of God!

2. We should take these words of God and store them in our hearts. Just as Luke was unashamed to tell His friend about who Jesus was, we should do the same. Let us go to our families, friends, and the world and proclaim Him as Christ!

3. We should remain steadfast and sure in our faith. It is an immovable, firm, unshakable, solid rock on which we should stand. As we begin this time of the Christmas season, may we fully rely on Christ for our hope, joy, and peace!

DECEMBER 4TH

Zechariah the Priest

Read:
Luke 1:5-11

DISCUSS

1. Why do all these different names and places mentioned in this passage matter?

2. Because Zechariah and Elizabeth were blameless, did this mean they had no sin?

3. Why are they burning incense in the temple, as mentioned in verse 9?

4. What is the significance of the Angel being on the right side of the altar, as mentioned in verse 11?

ANSWERS

1. All the names and places matter greatly in the grand narrative of the Bible. Genesis 3:15, "I will put enmity between you and the woman, and between your offspring and her offspring; he shall bruise your head, and you shall bruise his heel." We follow the line that comes from this offspring in order to fulfill this scripture in Genesis as we look to the coming Messiah!

2. This expression of blamelessness does not mean they did not sin. It just simply means that they were righteous and godly people, just as we should strive to be every day as we serve and follow the Lord. They served by faith to the coming Messiah. We serve by faith to the risen Messiah.

3. Incense symbolizes the prayers of God's people constantly ascending before the Lord. In the Tabernacle, incense could only be offered by the priests, who served as mediators; symbolically, they would bring their prayers into the presence of the Most High. Psalm 141:2, ESV, "Let my prayer be counted as incense before you, and the lifting up of my hands as the evening sacrifice!"

4. Where else in the Bible have we heard about the right side? That's right! Christ sitting at the right hand of the Father (Mark 16:19)! Some scholars can point to the right side being used to point to authority as Christ has authority over heaven and earth.

TAKEAWAYS

1. The story of the Bible is timeless and faultless. God will fulfill all he had promised in the coming days. God works in His own timing, and we can rest assured He keeps His promises.

2. We too can be blameless in the eyes of the Lord like Elizabeth and Zechariah. However, we can also seek to atone for our sins and be blameless as they were blameless in the faith of their sacrifices. We are made blameless by the bloodshed of the Savior on the Cross, who died for me and you.

3. Our prayers should be much like incense-never ceasing, lamenting, praises to our God. "Rejoice always, pray continually, give thanks in all circumstances; for this is God's will for you in Christ Jesus. Do not quench the Spirit. Do not treat prophecies with contempt but test them all; hold on to what is good," - 1 Thessalonians 5:16-21, ESV.

DECEMBER 5TH

Yahweh has Been Gracious

Read:
Luke 1:12-17

DISCUSS

1. What should verse thirteen teach us about prayer?

2. What, in the original language, does John's name mean?

3. What is the difference between Christ and John in the womb?

4. If many will rejoice at the birth of John, is he the Messiah?

5. What job has John been tasked with?

ANSWERS

1. We should learn from what the angel tells Zechariah. That God will answer our prayers in His timing and in His ways. We may get an answer to a prayer that is unexpected.. But, the Lord will answer prayers in ways that glorify Himself and not man.

2. John's name, according to the ESV Bible Commentary, means: YAHWEH has been gracious. This name is fitting for John as he will be the one who makes the proclamation of the one to come. He is going to show the people the One who will be the most gracious to them all by giving His life for all those who believe.

3. John is given the spirit of God in the womb. He is coming out ready and filled to complete the task that is given to him. Jesus in the womb is still God! He is not filled with a spirit; Jesus is fully God and fully human.

4. No! John is not the Messiah. John is the herald of the Messiah. This very fact is why many people will rejoice at John's birth. This is because, through John, all will know that the promised Messiah is coming soon!

5. John has been tasked with getting the people ready for Jesus. He is to herald and proclaim and shout from the mountaintops, "The Messiah is coming!"

TAKEAWAYS

1. Those of us filled with the spirit are given a command similar to John! We are to go out into the world and make disciples. This means we are to go forth into the world and tell others of the great news that Christ has come to seek and save!

2. Prayer is not meant to be used as a wish dispenser. Prayer is a way to talk with our Heavenly Father. God will, in His due time and way, make known to us the desires of our hearts. He will give us what we need and not what we want. Our wants and desires should one day fall in line with those of the Father.

3. Let us be careful to not make idols of people and things. We should be reminded that there is only one who can save, and that is Christ! He is calling upon His children to call upon His name! Do not be afraid to step out in faith and follow the creator of all things.

DECEMBER 6TH

Zechariah's Unfaithfulness

Read:
Luke 1:18-25

DISCUSS

1. Why is it wrong that Zechariah asked, "How shall I know this?"

2. What happened to Zechariah for his disbelief?

3. Did being silent prevent Zechariah from completing his job?

4. Why does Elizabeth keep herself hidden for five months?

5. What does Elizabeth mean when she talks about the Lord taking away her reproach among the people?

ANSWERS

1. We see that Zechariah asks this question,"How shall I know?" with disbelief. Well, he should know because the angel, Gabriel, standing in front of him, just told him the word of the Lord! Gabriel is in the presence of God when he speaks. The Lord has said these things, so they will be!

2. Zechariah was silenced, unable to speak until the things mentioned had come to pass. So, for nine months, Zechariah was unable to speak. I can't go five minutes without speaking; what a punishment!

3. No, verses 22-23, tell us that Zechariah keeps making signs to the people around him at the temple. Once his service as a priest at the temple was over, he went home.

4. It is thought among scholars that Elizabeth hid herself for five months in order to grow closer to the Lord. She stayed hidden in order to give praise and honor to God for finding favor with her.

5. Being a Jewish woman during this time, there was great pressure to bear children. Each woman looked forward to bearing children in hopes to be the mother of the Messiah. So, not having a child at all was seen as a punishment for some sort of sin. With this birth, God showed Elizabeth that she had His favor.

TAKEAWAYS

1. "The unbelief of man shall not make the promises of God of no effect, they shall be fulfilled in their season."[2] God works in His own time. Thankfully for Zechariah, the season happened to be very soon. We must take this as a reminder to ourselves. The Lord is working in our lives, whether we see it or not.

2. We should be careful when we question the word of God. God's word is truth; it will never cease. The word of God is still relevant and will always be so! When we begin to question the word of God we can easily fall into the sin of blasphemy.

3. Look at the word reproach. It effectively means an expression of disapproval and disappointment. As today's Christians, we need to be careful when we hear this idea of being right with the culture around us. They will never approve of us because we are different and seem weird. However, we are called to be above reproach, meaning do not be like the world!

DECEMBER 7TH

Birth of Jesus Foretold

Read:
Luke 1:26-33

DISCUSS

1. What did Mary do to gain favor with God?

2. Was Mary or Joseph from the lineage of the promised seed?

3. What is truly meant when we talk about "the throne of David"?

4. How will Jesus be great?

5. Should Jesus be remembered as the Son of Mary and Joseph or of the Most High God?

ANSWERS

1. Absolutely nothing; that is the beauty of the Gospel in which we proclaim. See, this was just one act out of many made in grace. Mary did not deserve such honor as to bring the King of the world into the Earth. Yet, God picked and used her anyway.

2. Joseph was, as stated in verse twenty-seven. Joseph was "Of the house of David." If this point interests you, go to the beginning of Matthew. Matthew clearly articulates the lineage of the promised seed coming to crush the head of the serpent.

3. Read 2 Samuel 7:12-16. We see that Christ will come to sit on a heavenly everlasting throne. Christ is to rule and reign over all creation. This is not a physical throne that we will see in our time here on earth, but a high priestly throne in heaven.

4. Jesus will be the great High Priest, Savior, Deliverer, and Shepherd. Jesus will be great in His obedience, and those He saves will be made righteous before God.

5. God ordained who would be the earthly parents of Jesus. However, it is most important to know that He has a heavenly Father, God. He is a part of the Triune God-Head. God the Father, the Son, and the Holy Spirit.

TAKEAWAYS

1. "Is it not proven that he is great? Conquerors are great, and He is the greatest of them. Deliverers are great, and He is the greatest of them. Liberators are great, and He is the greatest of them. Saviors are great, and He is the greatest of them."[3]

2. Be reminded that we have unmerited favor and grace upon us. If not for God, we would not be here today with breath in our lungs. We would not be able to sit around Christmas trees laden with presents without the grace of God.

3. Christ was brought into the world in one of the most humble ways. Mary and Joseph were not the richest. Yet, they were about to get the greatest treasure a parent could have–being a parent of the Son of the Most High.

DECEMBER 8TH

Mary's Submission

Read:
Luke 1:34-38

DISCUSS

1. What is the difference between how Zechariah reacted to the news from the angel and Mary?

2. Look to verse thirty-five, what do you find significant at the end of the verse?

3. Why do you think the angel told Mary about Elizabeth in verse 36?

4. If nothing is impossible with God, does this mean that we can get any present we want for Christmas?

5. What act do we see Mary perform in verse thirty-eight?

ANSWERS

1. Zechariah responded in disbelief to the word of God. However, Mary responded with disbelief in how she would bear the son of God. Look to verse forty-five and examine what Elizabeth tells Mary. Mary believed in the word of God. In contrast, look at what Zechariah says, "How will I know this?"

2. We see the angel say that Jesus will be "Called Holy - the Son of God." Many people will miss it, but this shows us Christ is God. It does not say that "He will become." Yet, it says, "He will be called." This helps point us to the Trinity and oneness with God the Father.

3. Gabriel, the angel, tells Mary about Elizabeth for two reasons. Firstly, to provide evidence that God can accomplish the "impossible." Secondly, it works to strengthen Mary's faith. How? Well, we, as believers, are satisfied with the word of God. However, seeing and hearing of a miracle performed by God works to strengthen the faith of God's children.

4. No! That is not what this verse means. We must be careful singling out a verse like this. We must read the word of God within the scope of the whole Bible! At this point in scripture, we see that the completion of the word of God is without fail, not God delivering our desires.

5. We see an act of submission. The Lord called Mary to be the mother of her Lord and ours. She graciously accepted and submitted to the will of the Father.

TAKEAWAYS

1. God the Son has been and always will be one with the Father and one with the Holy Spirit. There are not three separate Gods that we worship. Yet, there are three persons in one God. Since the beginning of time, He has been called "Son of God." He was never created or an afterthought. He always was God's plan of salvation.

2. "Though believers are satisfied with the bare word of God, yet they do not disregard any of His world which they find to be conducive to strengthen their faith."[4]

3. When we say that God is the God of impossible, or quote Philippians, "In Him I can do all things," we must be careful with taking the word of the Lord out of context. The Lord can supply and do many miraculous things in our lives but for His glory, not ours. Let us boast in what Christ has done, not in what we have done.

DECEMBER 9TH

Mary Visits Elizabeth

Read:
Luke 1:39-45

DISCUSS

1. In verse thirty-nine, what prompted Mary to visit her cousin Elizabeth?

2. What was the baby's name that "leaped" in Elizabeth's womb?

3. When Elizabeth cried out with a loud voice, why was she so filled with joy?

4. In verse forty-five, what were the keywords that Elizabeth spoke about Mary's faith?

5. Why is it significant that Elizabeth's baby would arrive six months before Mary's?

ANSWERS

1. When we read the Bible, we have to remember that it was not written in chapters but as one continuous letter. Read Luke 1:35-36. We can see that Mary goes forth in "haste" with the news of Elizabeth bearing a child from the angel Gabriel.

2. The baby in Elizabeth's womb is John, as mentioned earlier on day 5. Read Luke 1:13.

3. She was filled with the Holy Spirit, as mentioned in verse forty-one. Her joy was expressed through her worship. The baby, John, expressed joy in the best way he knew how. By leaping!

4. Mary was found blessed because she believed in what the angel of the Lord told her. We are most blessed in our lives when we trust in the promises of God.

5. The answer can be found in Luke 1:17. John would prepare the way by being the "forerunner" of Jesus Christ. See also Mark 1:2-4.

TAKEAWAYS

1. When Jesus lays a burden on our hearts to "go," we should do so. It will take faith and courage, but we must believe in what Jesus has called us to.

2. If we are a child of God and have come to the saving knowledge of Jesus Christ, the Third person of the Trinity resides in us. The Holy Spirit is entirely God.

3. Just as John the Baptist was the forerunner to tell people about the coming Messiah, we are the forerunners of the Gospel of Jesus Christ. This Christmas, think of someone you can share the Gospel with!

DECEMBER 10TH

Mary's Song of Praise

Read:
Luke 1:46-49

DISCUSS

1. What does it mean to magnify the Lord?

2. Who is Mary giving all this praise and glory to?

3. What great thing is God currently working on in Mary?

4. What should Mary's song teach us about how to celebrate Christmas?

5. Whose name is Holy?

ANSWERS

1. Magnify means to declare greatly and to exalt His name above all other things. Read Psalm 34 and see what the Psalter says about magnifying the name of the Lord. Use your time of get-togethers this year to magnify the Lord amongst all your friends and family members.

2. God the Father! She is singing praise to the one who just gave Mary the greatest news of salvation: the coming birth of the Messiah who she would bring into the world.

3. God is using Mary as the vessel to bring salvation unto the nation. Mary is not the Savior or a way to salvation. However, she is the earthly mother of Jesus. Nothing more, Nothing less. Let us be careful who we praise in this story–not Mary, but a good and gracious God.

4. It should teach us to praise God continually! What does Mary do once she hears the news of what's to come? She sings praises to the God of the universe in complete awe and reverence. Let us this season continue to tell of God's glory and perfection!

5. God! God is Holy. Holy is an important word to read upon. It is used 229 times in the New Testament alone. So, what does it mean for God to be Holy? God teaches us through His word that holy means to separate. God is separate or cut off from everything that is sinful and evil. God is not evil or sinful. There is not an ounce of this within His being. Therefore, He is the perfect image of holiness.

TAKEAWAYS

1. My spirit has rejoiced in God my savior (Luke 1:47). This means Mary knew that she needed a Savior, just as we need a Savior. May our hearts and souls come to know and rejoice in the great love and mercy of a Holy God.

2. "He who is mighty has done great things for me: This song mainly celebrates God's goodness, faithfulness, and power. Mary's song shows the futility of trusting in self, of trusting in political power, or of trusting in riches. Mary's trust was in God, and it was rewarded."[5]

3. During this busy season of life, remember to stop and look to the Savior–the reason we have cause to celebrate Christmas. Do not be worried by the things of everyday life, instead revel in the awe-inspiring word of God and look to the Holy One.

DECEMBER 11TH

Look Upon the Mercy of God

Read:
Luke 1:50-56

DISCUSS

1. What does it mean for someone to "fear" the Lord?

2. What are some things that the Lord has done with His strong arm as named in this song?

3. What are some ways God has shown mercy on the Israelites?

4. What are some ways God has shown mercy on you?

5. Does God speak to us like he did Abraham?

ANSWERS

1. In the Bible, fear is mostly used as a word to show reverence. Reverence is a feeling of awe or respect for someone or something. When we fear the Lord, we are in awe of His mighty nature and are giving Him His due respect. Within our fear of the Lord, we should act in obedience to His word.

2. The Lord is exalted here by doing the following:
    a. Scattering the proud
    b. Bringing down mighty kings
    c. Exalting those in humble estates
    d. Filling the hungry
    e. Sending the rich away empty handed
    f. Israel remembering His mercy and goodness

3. God has shown mercy to Israel in a multitude of ways:
    a. Freed them from slavery from Egypt
    b. Led them to the promised land
    c. Fed them water and mana in the wilderness
    d. Protected them from their enemies
    e. Showed mercy and grace when they easily turned away from His goodness and glory.

4. Parents, use this time to speak about how the Lord has been merciful to you! Help your children think of times that seemed really hard or stressful, yet the Lord brought them through it!

5. God does not speak to us as He did His people in the Old Testament. The way God speaks to us now is through His word in the Bible. We can no longer audibly hear the voice of God. However, all of His words and commands are given to us through the best book in all of existence, the Bible!

TAKEAWAYS

1. God is mighty and true. He deserves all honor, glory, and respect. We should fear the Lord and seek to obey His word every day.

2. Take this Christmas season to reflect on the mercies of God. We celebrate Christmas for the most ultimate mercy bestowed to man–the birth of the sinless Savior, who came and paid the debt we owed and brought us back to God.

3. There are several ways to never forget the goodness of God:
    a. Tell others about what He has done.
    b. Write about how He has worked in your life in a journal. You will be able to look back over it in a couple years and truly reflect on the goodness of God.
    c. Pray that you may never neglect or lose sight of God.

DECEMBER 12TH

The Birth of John the Baptist

Read:
Luke 1:57-66

DISCUSS

1. Do people who do not yet believe in God rejoice in His mercy?

2. Why did they want to call John, Zechariah?

3. Was John truly a baptist as we know the term today?

4. Why was Zechariah's tongue immediately loosened?

5. Why do all the people question who the child will be . . .don't they know?

ANSWERS

1. Yes, there are many ways that the Lord's mercy even extends to those who do not believe. The neighbors and family members were led to rejoice when they learned of the child Elizabeth bore. They knew she was unable to conceive a child. Yet, now she has one!

2. The historical custom of the day was to name the firstborn child after their fathers. It was a very weird thing that both John and Jesus were not named after their own fathers. Yet, this shows the change coming from salvation through faith in the coming Messiah, and faith in the accomplished work of the Messiah.

3. By no means! At this time in history, there were not several different denominations. He was called 'the baptist' due to the nature of his job, given by God. He came to pave the way towards the hope of the coming Messiah Jesus. He was baptizing people in the cause of repentance.

4. The angel said that Zechariah would be silent until the day that the things the angel mentioned took place. So, that means that Zechariah was to be silent until the birth and rightful naming of John was to happen. Thus, when Zechariah agreed to name the baby John, his tongue was loosened!

5. As a priest and servant of the temple Zechariah would have been familiar with the prophecies in Malachi. Especially the verses that speak of the one to come before the Messiah. So, the man who knew what was going to happen, thanks to the angel Gabriel, was unable to speak and tell anyone about what was happening. So, until the birth of John, many were confused about who this child was!

TAKEAWAYS

1. The Lord has bestowed mercy upon mercy onto his children. Namely those who believe. However, there are everyday moments of grace that are freely given even to those who do not believe or confess Christ as Lord and Savior.

2. God the Father is a promise keeper. He is not one to belabor a punishment or to withhold a blessing. He is the sustainer of working in His own timing what is best for His namesake and glory.

3. It's important to ask God to allow us to not be confused like the people around Zechariah and Elizabeth. I encourage you to be sure of the words that the Lord has given us through the Bible. May we hide these words in our heart and meditate on them day and night.

DECEMBER 13TH

Zechariah's Prophecy Part 1

**Read:
Luke 1:67-75**

DISCUSS

1. What does a prophecy mean?

2. What is the importance of prophecy in scripture?

3. What does it mean to be redeemed?

4. Who is the horn of salvation, and what is verse 69 representing?

5. How does God show mercy, and what is His holy covenant?

ANSWERS

1. Prophecy is to declare a message from God. It is a representation of something to take place in the future.

2. God's sovereignty is on full display when the prophets foretold something that would take place. Zechariah, who is filled with the Holy Spirit, tells the story of Christ, who through the lineage of David would be our salvation. God never makes a promise He doesn't keep. We can trust that Jesus who was foretold throughout the Old Testament is enough!

3. Redeem means to buy back. We have redemption through Christ, who shed His blood on the cross so that we may be brought back to God through His son. See Ephesians 1:7 and Galatians 3:13.

4. The horn here signifies something or someone strong and powerful. Read Psalm 18:2. The Lord is our deliverer and our salvation. This verse represents Jesus who alone is to be praised.

5. Mercy is to withhold something. Romans 6:23 tells us that the wages of sin is death. We are subjected to the wrath of God because of our sinful nature not upholding the Old Covenant. God, in His mercy, withheld His wrath on us and poured it out on His son. The free gift of God is eternal life in Christ Jesus our Lord. This is the New Covenant that is the perfect promise from God. See Hebrews 9:15.

TAKEAWAYS

1. Be careful not to listen to "God told me" stories today that falsely add to Scripture. We as Christians should understand that God has given us what we need already in His word. Salvation is found in Christ and Christ alone.

2. Continue reading Psalm 18. What an amazing reminder that the Lord is our salvation. We have been delivered and bought with a price. Just like David in this Psalm, let there be the praise and worship in our hearts this season.

3. Not only did God show mercy by withholding His wrath on us, He offers grace as a free gift. This can only happen through the finished work of Jesus on the cross.

DECEMBER 14TH

Zechariah's Prophecy Part 2

**Read:
Luke 1:76-80**

DISCUSS

1. Who is it in verse seventy-six that John the Baptist will go before to tell of?

2. How is it that one might be saved according to verse seventy-seven?

3. Why do you think the word tender is used in verse seventy-eight?

4. According to verse seventy-nine, what is the way of peace?

ANSWERS

1. This verse references Jesus and is a clear proclamation that Jesus is Lord. This is foundational to the Christian faith. Jesus is not just a prophet, healer, or good person. He is God in flesh. He is the radiance of the glory of God and the exact imprint of His nature as described in Hebrews 1:3.

2. Read Mark 1:4 and John 1:7. Salvation is found in Christ and Christ alone. John was to bear witness of Christ and to proclaim that through faith and repentance, one might be saved.

3. The CSB translation uses the word "compassion." We serve a tender, compassionate God. He loves us so much that He sent His one and only Son to be our substitute. Only God can be this gentle. The word tender here magnifies how merciful He really is.

4. According to John 8:12, Jesus is the light of the world and life is found in the light. The only way to have true peace with God is to know Christ as your Savior. For in verse 79, it says that Christ, being the light, will "guide our feet to the way of peace."

TAKEAWAYS

1. We can all learn from the ministry of John the Baptist and how important it is for us to give knowledge to people of how they might be saved. Plant the seed of the gospel with someone today!

2. It is impossible to find our way in the dark. We must have a light to see where we are going. Read Matthew 5:14-16. Pray that the light of Christ shines in our lives wherever we go.

3. Take a moment to reflect on how God has been merciful to you in your life. What a mighty, compassionate God we serve!

DECEMBER 15TH

Joseph's Righteousness

Read:
Matthew 1:18-19

DISCUSS

1. What does the name of Jesus mean?

2. Why did Joseph want to divorce Mary quietly?

3. Why would Mary be put to shame?

4. What does this say about the character of Joseph?

5. Can you see God working out His plan of salvation in this situation?

ANSWERS

1. The name of Jesus is Greek for the name Joshua. Thus the name means, "YAHWEH Saves".[6] Why is His name to be called Jesus? He shall save people from their sins.

2. Joseph did not want to put Mary into a spotlight by openly divorcing her. Divorce is not a suitable thing to engage in. However, the Lord put it in place to protect those involved. Joseph did not want to shame Mary by making an example of her in public.

3. If Joseph divorced Mary publicly, it would have put the blame on Mary. It would make it look like Mary cheated on Joseph when she did not. She was gifted the baby Jesus by the Holy Spirit.

4. Look at what the scriptures say about him. It says he was "a just man." This points to Joseph being a righteous man and one looked out for others before himself. God knew what He was doing by picking Mary and Joseph to be the parents of Jesus!

5. Look at how God has begun to work once more in the lives of those He seeks to save. He knew the heart of Joseph. He knew the questions of Mary and the unbelief of Zechariah. He also knew of the great love and praise that would come from both Mary and Elizabeth.

TAKEAWAYS

1. God is sovereign. Which means that God is in control of all things in heaven, and on earth, and under the earth. Everything that happens, happens for His goodwill and pleasure.

2. The word of God is infallible. This means that the word of God is trustworthy and is without error. The words found in our Bible have been safeguarded without error for thousands of years.

3. God is omnipotent. God is without an end to his power or authority. There is nothing that overrules or overrides it. All power and authority belongs to God. No other idols, human beings, or gods will ever take that from Him.

DECEMBER 16TH

God With Us

Read:
Matthew 1:20-25

DISCUSS

1. Which major prophet spoke the words quoted in verse twenty-three?

2. What does the name Immanuel mean?

3. What is the significance of the name?

4. What does verse twenty show us about God's knowledge and wisdom?

5. If they were to call Him Immanuel, where did the name Jesus come from?

ANSWERS

1. Isaiah 7:14 is who/what is being quoted. The New Testament writers frequently quoted this prophet, often showing how his prophecies pointed not just to the Israelites' redemption from exile but to the world's redemption in Christ! Isaiah was used by God in a mighty way to point us to something greater than ourselves.

2. The name Immanuel means God with us. This is to point to the coming One–the Messiah, savior of the world, prince of peace, and everlasting Father.

3. This word is significant as it points to Christ, who is a person within the God-head trinity. God the Son has come in flesh to be fully man and fully God and to serve as a payment for our sins.

4. This verse helps show us something very important. God knows our heart, hears our thoughts, and knows our very desires. When we have no idea what to say in prayer, the Lord knows and is working to make all things new. He went to Joseph to reassure him this was his task at hand, let's see it to completion!

5. Immanuel is not a personal name. In Isaiah 7:14, it is seen as fulfilled, not in the naming of Jesus, but in the whole account of His origin and naming. It is not that Jesus ever bore the name Immanuel but that it indicates His role: bringing God's presence to man and Christ becoming flesh.

TAKEAWAYS

1. God is the one whom we should adore and give all praise. God is the one who knows all things in heaven and on earth. We can not hide anything from the sight of God.

2. Immanuel, God with us. God the Son came and lived among His people and lived a sinless life. He is now ruling and reigning over all the earth. Let us remember what He has accomplished this season as we go and tell others of His great name.

3. Obedience is of importance when serving God. We can not seek to serve man and God, as we can only serve the God man, Christ. As you begin to meditate on the words of the Lord, allow Him to open your eyes and heart. Allow Him to show you those around you who are lost and dying and speak words of life to them. How can they hear if no one goes?

DECEMBER 17TH

The Birth of Jesus Christ

Read:
Luke 2:1-7

DISCUSS

1. In verse one when it says all the world, did Augustus truly mean the entire world?

2. We are just a verse or two away from the birth, what is important about the town of Bethlehem?

3. What economic product does Bethlehem Ephrathah produce?

4. What is the significance behind Jesus being born and placed into a manger?

5. There was no place for them in the inn. What do you think this rejection later points to?

ANSWERS

1. No! They did not know that there was a vast whole world around them. They did not have the technology to travel. "The world," meant all that Rome was ruling over.

2. Look to Michah 5:2! What does it say? It says that the Messiah will be born there. We see that God is already setting into place His plan and the fulfillment of a prophecy!

3. Historically, this Bethlehem was known for breeding and producing sheep that were used for sacrifices to God. However, they did not know they were about to house and give life to the most important sacrificial lamb of all, Christ Jesus our Lord.

4. Well, we see that the God of the universe came to the world, fully God and fully man, with the purpose of living with His people and caring for them. Christ lived a perfect, sinless life, and He lived in some of the poorest, humblest positions.

5. This points to the later rejection we will see at the end of Jesus' life. He will soon be rejected by the very people He came to save. Jesus faced rejection His whole life! From birth to death, the world did not want what He truly came to do. They sought for an earthly king, not a heavenly king.

TAKEAWAYS

1. God has once again proven His sovereignty in all things. What a cool way to really drive home the idea of Christ being the ultimate sacrificial lamb. By not only having Him be born amongst the sheep but in the town where sacrificial sheep were born!

2. Reflect on the words of Hebrews 2:5-8. Look to the humbleness of Christ in regard to the love He has for those He came to seek and save.

3. Increasingly today, many will be rejected for celebrating Christmas rightly. What I mean is, when we put emphasis on the Savior and not the presents, people who don't know Jesus yet will not understand. Do not let the culture pressure you into caring more about the physical presents than the heavenly one given in Christ Jesus our Lord.

DECEMBER 18TH

Shepherd's and Angels

Read:
Luke 2:8-14

DISCUSS

1. These scriptures take place in what region? ?

2. Why do you think people were filled with fear whenever angels appeared? Aren't they meant to be beautiful?

3. What is the "Good news of great joy"?

4. What day was Jesus born?

5. What is so cool about "a multitude of hosts praising God"?

ANSWERS

1. We are still in Bethlehem, the city of David. The shepherds are still in the fields attending to the sheep. These are the sheep that will be used for sacrifices in the temple. However, they are about to learn of the greatest sacrificial lamb to grace Earth!

2. Look to other scriptures in the Bible, what do they say about the angels? Are they more scary looking or beautiful to look at? See Daniel 10:5-6; Revelation 10:1; Revelation 4:8; Ezekiel 10:14.

3. Read verse eleven! A savior. Christ the Lord is born! Amen and Hallelujah! What an awesome message!

4. We cannot confidently say that Jesus was born on December 25th. However, "The date we now call Christmas is the most ancient recorded date that the church has celebrated. In the 2nd century AD we find a Western church leader named Hippolytus, wrote a strong argument for the December 25th date."[7]

5. If you look at the historical meaning of the word "hosts," it usually refers to an army. An army does not typically stand for peace. It usually stands for war and defense. So, to see that an entire army of angels was declaring peace over the earth must have been a sight to see!

TAKEAWAYS

1. There is one phrase that I do not like being used, and that is "remember the reason for the season." It is a great reminder. However, no one ever expounds on what the reason is. Remember that the reason for this season is Christ, the incarnate son of God, who came to seek and save the multitudes of lost, dying, and sinful people!

2. Angels were used as messengers of the word of God. They are not to be worshiped or revered as anything more than what they are. Their objective is to point others to the Messiah and God. We should seek to be heralders of the word!

3. Take this time to reflect on your "shepherd," or in a more literal sense, pastor. He takes his time every week to sit and meditate over the word of God in order to accurately preach a clear message of redemption over his flock. You, his people and sheep.

> DECEMBER 19TH

Jesus' Birth Proclaimed

**Read:
Luke 2:15-18**

DISCUSS

1. Why did the shepherds go straight to Bethlehem?

2. What is so important about verse sixteen regarding the birth of Jesus?

3. Look at verse seventeen at the phrase "When they had seen." Why is this important to the message that the shepherds would tell?

4. How were the shepherds the first missionaries to share the good news of the gospel of Jesus Christ?

5. Consider the people who "heard" the shepherd's message . . . why did they wonder?

ANSWERS

1. They had faith that God himself had spoken to them through the angel of the Lord.

2. The words spoken by the angel in verse 2:12 came to pass as the angel said it would. The shepherds had faith without seeing before they ever arrived in Bethlehem.

3. The shepherds would be the first eyewitnesses (other than Mary and Joseph) to the message they accepted by faith but would later verify with their eyes. Read 2 Peter 1:16.

4. The shepherds were the first to go and share what they had heard and seen.

5. They wondered for many reasons, but here are two:
    a. They were not eyewitnesses
    b. They lacked "faith" in the message the shepherds shared.

TAKEAWAYS

1. Each of us is given faith by the Holy Spirit. The Holy Scriptures are the voice of God. Each of us should feel eagerness to go forth and tell of His goodness–to make disciples of all nations.

2. When we share the good news of the Gospel, we have numerous eyewitnesses that give proof of Jesus Christ's birth and resurrection. The evidence is in the Bible. We are justified by faith. Romans 5:1

3. You will meet people in life who, when you share the good news of Jesus Christ, will hear you but not respond. They will continue to wonder. Our calling is to share and teach, not convince and convert.

DECEMBER 20TH

Jesus Presented at the Temple

Read:
Luke 2:19-24

DISCUSS

1. What things are Mary still pondering in verse nineteen?

2. Where did the shepherds return to?

3. Do you think that the shepherds sang praises out loud or inside their heads?

4. What does verse twenty-one teach us about faithful obedience?

5. Where does verse twenty-two point us to in the Old Testament?

ANSWERS

1. Look to verse seventeen. The shepherds were relaying what the angels had told them. "Glory to God in the highest, and on earth peace among those with whom He is pleased!" The savior of the world was born! What a great and solid confirmation for what has just occurred in the lives of Mary and Joseph.

2. They must have returned to the fields in which they were tending to the sheep. Now, one or two things happened with the sheep. One, the shepherds left the sheep there by themselves or took the sheep with them to Jesus. The Bible does not explicitly tell us what they did. However, imagine them rushing away from their job because of the message and news that the Messiah had come!

3. The shepherds went all the way back to the fields, singing and praising out loud! Imagine how weird this sight may have been for those in the streets. To see nasty, smelly shepherds singing (most likely off-key) about the birth of the Savior. What a sight that must have been. See, we should look like those weird shepherds and continually sing praises and share the message that our Christ came for us and to all people!

4. It could be so easy to follow the traditions of your family than to follow the commands of the Lord. Instead of going against the Lord and naming Jesus a family name, they stayed true in faithful obedience to God the Father and named that sweet baby Jesus.

5. Leviticus 12:2-6. What does this mean for us today? Well, this shows us that Jesus and those born around the same time were one of the last ones to do this ritual to make

the mother and child clean. Because of this child born in Bethlehem, we no longer need to follow this law of purification!

TAKEAWAYS

1. We should treat the word of God as Mary has in these verses. She took the word of the Lord and stored it in her heart. She treasured it and pondered upon it. We should seek to do the same with the word of God today. We should hide His word in our heart, so we do not sin against it.

2. Do not let family traditions run your life. Instead, let the word of the Lord be the basis of your family's faith and foundation. Do not just merely go to church because your family does it. Go to church because you have a desire to worship a holy and just God.

3. When you come to church and when you go to work, be like the shepherds and give all glory, honor, and praise to your heavenly Father. Sing of the greatness of our savior, no matter how you sound, look or smell. Praise God continually in all that you do. May the praises of the Lord never cease from your lips.

DECEMBER 21ST

Behold Our Salvation

Read:
Luke 2:25-32

DISCUSS

1. What does "bringing consolation to Israel" mean?

2. How did Simeon receive the Holy Spirit before Christ sent Him to earth?

3. Why is Simeon blessing God for allowing him to depart in peace?

4. What does Simeon mean in verse 30 by, "See your salvation"?

5. Look deeper: what prophecy is being fulfilled here in verse thirty-two?

ANSWERS

1. The word consolation here means something more than what we hear on TV. We might be more familiar with the word consolation as a prize after losing. This is a little different; the word here actually means comfort. This is the comfort the Israelites would receive after the coming of Christ, which, here in the chapter, is so close to completion!

2. The Holy Spirit was able to come upon Simeon for a very special reason. Simeon was known as a prophet of the Lord–someone who would proclaim the coming of Christ. Simeon would be one of the last recorded prophets who would proclaim the coming of the Savior!

3. Let us look back to verse 2:26. We see that the Lord told Simeon he would not see death until He sent His Son, the Messiah and Prince of Peace. This of course, means when he sees Jesus!

4. This phrase points to the child who would bring God's salvation to all of humanity. Simeon is speaking of the One who would come to seek and save the lost here on earth.

5. Look to Isaiah 49:6. Christ and His mighty work on the cross to save sinners like me and you was and is meant to be used as a gospel light. This light will go forth till the end of days, proclaiming salvation to those who seek the Lord and proclaim Him as Lord and Savior. We must go and tell others of Christ!

TAKEAWAYS

1. There is only one place and one person that we should look to for our salvation. That is the very one Simeon was talking about. The Christ, the Messiah, the Lord of Lords and King of Kings . . .Jesus Christ!

2. Here we see an amazing thing taking place. We see the fulfillment of two prophecies! We can see this throughout the entire narrative of Christ being born. What an outstanding thing to witness. We are blessed with the ability to look back through all of time and see the prophecies being fulfilled one by one.

3. There is only one light, one comforter, that we must seek. That is Christ Himself! As it says in His word, Jesus said to Him, "I am the way and the truth and the life. No one goes to the Father except through me." - John 14:6

DECEMBER 22ND

Mary Had a Little Lamb

Read:
Luke 2:33-35

EXTRA READING

In 1877, Thomas Edison invented the phonograph. We call this the record player. He decided to test the new phonograph with a nursery rhyme that went like this: "Mary had a little lamb whose fleece was white as snow, and everywhere that Mary went, the Lamb was sure to go. It followed her to school one day, which was against the rule, and made the children laugh and play to see the lamb at school." This was the first recording of a human voice in history. Many people believe this nursery rhyme is telling the story of Jesus, and today, I want us to find the connections between this rhyme and our Bible reading for today.

DISCUSS

1. Who does the lamb represent in the story?

2. Why does the lamb have a fleece as white as snow?

3. Think about Mary in the song of the Bible. Where was she going with the Lamb?

4. Why was it against the rules of the day for Mary to have Jesus?

5. Why was it a problem for the children to laugh and play at school?

ANSWERS

1. Jesus

2. Jesus was born without sin!

3. Bethlehem!

4. Because Herod did not want any other king of the Jews!

5. Because it was upsetting the plans of the school. In the same way, Jesus upset the plans of Herod, the Pharisees, and the kingdoms of this world!

TAKEAWAYS

1. 1. In Luke 2:34 Simeon says, "This child is appointed for the fall and rising of many in Israel, and for a sign that is opposed." When Jesus appears on the scene, many people will rise (believe) and many people will fall (not believe). Many will oppose the sign of the cross, that God sent His Son to pay for their sins.

2. 2. In verse 35, Simeon says, "A sword will pierce your own soul also." What was going to be so hard about Mary having this little lamb, Jesus? One day, Mary was going to have to look upon her own Son, the Lamb of God who takes away the sin of the world, being crucified and dying on the cross. Mary was there watching the whole time. Do you think Mary was very sad or very glad when Jesus was on the Cross?

3. 3. In verse 35, Simeon says, "So that the thoughts from many hearts may be revealed." What Jesus did on the cross reveals what is in our hearts. For some people, they see Jesus on the cross, and they mock Him, because they believe they are good enough to get to heaven without Jesus. For other people, they see Jesus on the cross, and they know they deserved death because of their own sin. These are the people who believe in Jesus. They believe that Jesus was the Lamb, born of Mary, to take away the sin of the world.

DECEMBER 23RD

Anna the Prophetess

Read:
Luke 2:36-38

DISCUSS

1. Why do you think Luke mentions the prophetess Anna's age? How does this help fill out these verses?

2. Similarly, why does Luke mention that Anna was a widow of 84 years?

3. Anna serves as the final person to respond in Luke 2 to the birth of Jesus, what does her response reveal about the importance of Jesus' birth?

4. Why does Anna thank God for the birth of Jesus Christ? How is Jesus the redemption of Jerusalem?

5. What can we learn from Anna's response in regard to how we should respond to the birth of Jesus Christ?

ANSWERS

1. For many years, Anna had been in the temple, serving, fasting, and praying. Interestingly, she is a prophetess, someone who is prophesying about what is to come for Israel. I imagine much of her prophecy centered on the coming Messiah. And behold, after such a long life, the Messiah has been born, and in an instant, all of her prayers, fasting, and work found its fulfillment. Imagine hoping and praying for the Messiah to come and to do this well into your twilight years just to see Him. Pure joy.

2. Interestingly, the text also states that she had been a widow for 84 years. Another dimension of the yearning she had been feeling is added. Not only was this birth her greatest expectation, but also her greatest comfort. She had no one but the redemption of Jerusalem that had just arrived. This should be connected back to verse twenty-five, where Jesus is called Israel's consolation. He is the comfort and hope of Israel, for He is their redemption.

3. This response reveals a lot about the importance of the birth of Jesus. Firstly, it introduces the theme of redemption. This theme calls back to the exodus, where God redeemed His people out of Egypt. Now, God is going to redeem His people out of a greater foe, sin. Furthermore, this text shows that the birth of Jesus is great news to everyone, including an elderly widow who had dedicated her life to God's temple.

4. Anna thanks God for Jesus because He is "Him to all who were looking." God has been faithful to His promises. All of His promises that a Messiah was coming have now been fulfilled in the birth of Jesus. Moreover, redemption for Je-

rusalem (or Israel) has now arrived. Israel's true salvation has come. The world's true salvation has come!

5. Give thanks for the Messiah who has come. God has shown His faithfulness and has given his Son to us. May we look forward to His second coming in the same way Anna does. If Christ returns while we are well advanced in age, may we, in that moment give thanks to God for our hope is here! But let us follow Anna's example today and pray the prayer I am sure she prayed, "Come, Lord Jesus!" (Revelation 22:20). Let us look back with joy that redemption has arrived in Christ Jesus while we look forward with great anticipation to His second coming.

TAKEAWAYS

1. Anna's response concludes the series of responses we have read to the birth of Jesus. She rounds out the response that we ought to have with thanksgiving and hope. Today, are you thankful for Jesus' birth? Today, do you have the hope that Anna had realized with her eyes?

2. Be encouraged by Anna's example: may we live a life wholly dedicated to Jesus. It ought to be easier for us as He has already come once. She worked, prayed, and fasted daily yearning and desiring for Jesus Christ. Then, when He appeared, she was complete. May we live in such a way. May we yearn and desire Jesus with sincerity. May we be found complete in Him. May He be our greatest joy and life's ambition.

3. Lastly, we learn how to look forward to the second coming of Christ. Just as Anna worked until the first coming of

Jesus we ought to work hard too. May we be dedicated to the task that God has prepared before us. Anna prophesied about the hope to come; she told people to look forward too. May we in a similar way tell people about Jesus the one they must look to for hope. And may we not be slow in doing this. For He is coming SOON INDEED!

DECEMBER 24TH - *CHRISTMAS EVE*

Jesus Returns to Nazareth

Read:
Luke 2:39-40

DISCUSS

1. Why did Mary and Joseph perform everything according to the Law of the Lord?

2. Jesus and His family returned to Nazareth . . . why is this significant?

3. Jesus would grow in wisdom. Since Jesus was God, why does Luke tell us He grew in wisdom? Wouldn't He already be wise?

4. Jesus became strong, not only physically but also spiritually. Why is this important?

5. Do we receive the same grace that Jesus received?

ANSWERS

1. Jesus did not come to break God's law but to fulfill it (Matthew 5:17).

2. Jesus would be called a "Nazarene." In the ancient script, Jesus was at times referred to as Jesus of Nazareth. Remember that both Joseph and Mary lived in Nazareth before they made their journey to Bethlehem. Acts 2:22

3. We must remember that Jesus was 100% God but also 100% man. He would learn and experience God just like any man would. Although He had a divine nature, He would learn and experience everything just like us.

4. Because He was entirely man, He would grow in His knowledge and love for the Father as a human. The Holy Spirit would be with Jesus the same way He is always here for us. Jesus would have to be physically, mentally, and spiritually strong to endure what He did for us by dying on the cross for our sins.

5. Yes, the grace that Jesus was given would be the same grace that Jesus gives to us (John 1:16-17).

TAKEAWAYS

1. We as Christians must strive to keep the law but must understand that by the grace and mercy of Jesus Christ, we are not condemned when we fail the law. We must realize it is the work of Christ, not our work, that saves us.

2. Jesus knows how we feel. He experienced all the emotions we have. Why can we say this? Because He is God in the flesh. He is fully God and man.

3. Rest in the assurance that the grace and mercy that Jesus received, we can receive as well. The Spirit of the Lord in Jesus is the same Spirit that resides in us.

DECEMBER 25TH
CHRISTMAS DAY!

Word Became Flesh

Read:
John 1:14-16

DISCUSS

1. Go back to verses 1-5 in John–who is this Word?

2. The other Gospels record Jesus' name as Immanuel (God with us). What is the significance of the Word (God) dwelling among us?

3. The glorious Son comes to dwell among us and He is full of grace and truth. What message is being conveyed in these two words, grace and truth?

4. Notice the grace in the incarnation, grace upon grace. How does the simple fact that Jesus was born on this day show grace?

5. How can you celebrate today the Word that was made flesh and dwelt among us?

ANSWERS

1. The word is Jesus, God the Son. He is the one from the beginning by whom all things were made. He is God eternal, and in Him alone is the life and light of man.

2. It is the word that has been made flesh and has dwelt among us. God eternal, the one whom all things came into being, has now entered into creation through the humble means of being born a baby in a manger. Man has lived in darkness but the light of the world has now entered into it, and the darkness can only run from it. It is in the fact that God is with us that we can have hope. The Messiah has been born, and God Himself will settle what is wrong with the world. This all starts with the birth of Jesus.

3. John here summarizes what it means for God to be with us. Jesus is full of grace. In Jesus there is grace for us sinners. There is now hope for us rebels, for Christ has broken onto the scene, and salvation is here. Also, Jesus is full of truth. This message is not too good to be true, but it is the truth. All of history and the point of all things are fulfilled in Jesus. He himself is the point of all things, and this truth has dawned on humanity this Christmas day.

4. Praise the Lord, Jesus is born! Normally, we sing songs about Jesus' work, death, and resurrection for good reason. However, grace upon grace began this day. God needed nothing, yet it was His will to save sinners. And he does this by sending the Son, who humbly takes upon Himself our humanity and serves as a servant. Without the incarnation, we have no hope; Jesus had to come, and He had to come as a human. Because Jesus was born today, we know that we have received grace upon grace.

5. Go to church on Sunday. Praise the one who has dwelt among us. It is only in the birth of Jesus Christ that we have hope. He has come, and through Him, we have received grace upon grace. Let us go give thanks, for Christ has come, and God is with us! Salvation is here!

TAKEAWAYS

1. God dwelt among us in God the Son, incarnate; Jesus Christ. Jesus is God eternal and He is human in every way that you and I are human. Yet, He is the spotless Lamb, without sin. It is this Lamb who was born in Bethlehem on this day in History who will take away the sin of the world. So today, worship for the Lamb was slain for you (John 1:29).

2. In Jesus, we know all truth and have received grace upon grace. Jesus is not just the reason for the season, but He is the reason for all existence, both in creation and redemption. Everything centers on Him. And praise the Lord, it does! For in Him we have received grace upon grace, and through Him, we have forgiveness of our sins and eternal life with God (Ephesians 1:7). So today, meditate on the grace of the incarnation.

3. Today is Christmas. We will have presents to open, meals to savor, and family to enjoy. But may we give special attention to our Lord and Savior who was born in the manger today, for there is no better way to spend Christmas than worshiping the one through whom we have hope. The true present is Jesus, God with us. The true fulfillment is His grace and truth. Lastly, the true joy is the light of the world who dwelt among us. May you have a wonderful Christmas day. The word dwells among us, praise the Lord! Jesus the Christ was born today!

Notes

1. Henry, Matthew. 2003. Matthew Henry's Concise Commentary on the Whole Bible. N.p.: Thomas Nelson Incorporated.

2. "He Shall be Great." n.d. The Spurgeon Library. Accessed July 2, 2024. https://www.spurgeon.org/resource-library/sermons/he-shall-be-great/#flipbook/.

3. Calvin, John. n.d. "Work info: Commentary on Matthew, Mark, Luke - Volume 1." Christian Classics Ethereal Library. Accessed July 2, 2024. https://ccel.org/ccel/calvin/calcom31/calcom31.

4. "Enduring Word Bible Commentary Luke Chapter 1." n.d. Enduring Word. Accessed July 2, 2024. https://enduringword.com/bible-commentary/luke-1/.

5. "Jesus Arrived At The Perfect Time | Discover the Book Ministries." 2018. Discover the Book Ministries | Accessed July 2, 2024.

6. https://dtbm.org/jesus-arrived-at-the-perfect-time/.

7. "Strong's Greek: 2424. Ἰησοῦς (Iésous) -- Jesus or Joshua, the name of the Messiah, also three other Isr." n.d. Bible Hub. Accessed September 4, 2024. https://biblehub.com/greek/2424.htm.

About the Author

Dakota Stephens is a Southern Baptist pastor passionate about proclaiming God's Word and equipping others for discipleship. He serves as the family ministry pastor at Friendship Southern Baptist Church in North Carolina. There he partners with parents to train up children in the way of the Lord. In addition to his pastoral ministry, he enjoys writing, podcasting with fellow Reformed Baptist pastors, and hosting creative events that build up the community. When he's not serving the church, Pastor Dakota is a dedicated husband to his beautiful wife Holly, and father to his two son's Hank and Teddy. He currently attends full time at Judson College, the extension of Southeastern Baptist Theological Seminary. He is currently set to graduate with his B.A in Pastoral Ministry in 2026. He resides in Albemarle, NC and seeks to savor the blessings of family life with every moment the Lord grants him.

www.ingramcontent.com/pod-product-compliance
Lightning Source LLC
Chambersburg PA
CBHW070152080526
44586CB00015B/1956